Open Mick's Lyrical Bollards

Sean Byrne

William Cornelius Harris Publishing

In collaboration with

London Poetry Books

ISBN 978-1-911232-67-4

14 Fairlawn 159 Kingsway Hove

W
C
H
P

London Poetry Books

Dedication

For my brother Jimmy 1955 - 2025

Contents

Open Mick's Lyrical Bollards

POETRY TART

I fell in love with the game from the start
Always destined to be a football tart,
Not a great athlete, you might say puny
But I ran around like a bit of a looney.

Played for teams all over town
But never got picked when the scouts came down,
In the semi-final I missed a sitter
Could've been a contender but I'm not bitter.

I did get an offer from Walton and Hersham
But I stuck out for the big league, that's my version,
Soon found out I was not in the frame
But was still infatuated by the beautiful game.

A utility player, I didn't care
I'd turn out for anyone, anywhere
I never worked out the coaches' lingo False
No. 9, could've been bingo.

Inverted full-back? Might've been French
Spent a fair bit of time on the bench,
But I jumped into action when they gave me a start
That's why they call me a football tart.

As I got older the joints got stiff
I started to wonder what if? what if?
I was clever with words though you'd hardly know it
Maybe I could be a performance poet.

I saw an advert for open mic{k}
No way mate, that sounds sick,
You can't stand up there making jokes
About the idiosyncrasies of Irish folks.

I got that wrong but now I'm ok
Open miking almost every day,
When I get heckled I don't give up hope
I'd go to the opening of an envelope.

I might take a while to master the art
Here's to the trainee poetry tart.

PLASTIC PADDY POWER

The canals and the bridges, the embankments and cuts
They blasted and dug with their sweat and their guts,
Sing Kevin Barry and The Irish Rover
To keep you sane as you build the flyover.

A punt in the bookies, then a few beers
Then back on the road with McAlpine's fusiliers,
Buy a bri-nylon shirt every Friday night
But you'll have to bin it if you get into a fight.

Get all spruced up for the Saturday dance
Shake a good leg and you might have a chance,
Women on one side, men on the other
Who's gonna be the first to break cover?

Some strike lucky, others get arseholed
From Kilburn and Cricklewood to the Dublin Castle,
Get carried away when you've had a good session
Then wipe the slate clean when you go to confession.

Lay your head down in what digs you can find
No dogs, blacks or Irish at the back of your mind,
At the Tropicana you can throw a few shimmies
Or next to the Bedford there's a dive they call Jimmy's.

They'd sing rebel songs and pass round the hat
Who's the money for? Don't ask about that
After the fun, time to settle down
Raise a big family in old London town.

Kids sent off to the Catholic school
Those priests are sadistic, so don't play the fool,
Some grew up wild, some lasted the pace
Some travelled the world, we're a wandering race.

Others succeeded through education
Look to the future, maybe once more a nation,
Kept hold of our passports, it seemed a safe bet
While they voted for Brexit, how dumb can you get?

Now the empire is crumbling by the day by the hour
Maybe it's time for Plastic Paddy Power.

WHERE ARE YOU FROM?

'Where are you from?' asked the lady from the palace
'But where are you really from?' she said without malice

'I can't see your badge. Let me move your hair
Are you on the level? Are you on the square?'

'Are you really English with a name like Fulana?
You must be from Africa, somewhere like Ghana'

And now it's the Euros, we all shout at the telly
Step up to the spot and give it some welly.

You're ok if you score, we won't make a fuss
But if you slip up, you're not one of us.

You score, you're a hero, if not you're a slacker
And what kind of name is Bukayo Saka?

We're in it together, all part of the team
But can you be English with a name like Raheem?

Then up steps Harry, whacks it over the bar
He'll have an Irish granny if you go back that far.

'So, where were you born? Let's hear your version'
'Just outside London in a village called Hersham'

'I'm not being nosey, just having a chat
But where were you really born? Born before that?'

THE MAN WITH A SHELL UP HIS ARSE

Old Jean-Claude woke up in pain
Felt his innards going down the drain,
He went to a clinic a mile down the road
He felt something there about to explode.

The docs sat him down and sprang into action
Got out the forceps and performed an extraction,
When it was done, they stood back in awe
A thirteen inch shell from the 2nd world war.

A medical phenomenon, Quelle finesse, quelle classe
Respect for the man with the shell up his arse,
A local hero, he basked in the glory
Was offered good money for his side of the story.

How did it happen? It's anyone's guess
Maybe a prank in the officers' mess,
He joined the resistance and fought for the French
Maybe he got it when he sat in the trench.

Or could it have been a German howitzer?
Up the derriere and hasta la vista,
Quel age avez-vous? J'ai quatre-vigant cinq
Bright as a button, thick as a plank.

Vive la France et toujours la gloire!
You must have been seven when you fought in that war,
Looks like the accident must be more recent
Just track your movements and please make it decent.

The nation awaits, don't tarnish our glory
Just give us the details and we'll clean up the story,
It's out in the open, a big song and dance
Pass the ammunition et vive la France.

REPLACEMENT BUS

24 minutes from Tulse Hill
We're turfed the train
They ushered us off
To wait in the rain
It's under control
So don't make a fuss
Form an orderly queue
For the replacement bus.

Sat next to a geezer
Who looked a bit leery
Got GBH of the earhole
As he set out his theory
Replacement's the danger
It's all the rage
Keep 'em all out
Or locked in a cage.

They come over here
And take all our jobs
Live on the dole
And act like yobs
They breed like rabbits
And want to take over
Replacement boats at the
White cliffs of Dover.

Across the pond
Supremacy's in danger
President howling like
A dog in the manger
Another brick in the wall
From Lego or Meccano
We don't have room
For one more Chicano.

If they knock it down
And the bricks start to fall
We'll build another
Replacement wall
We dealt with the Indians
Without too much fuss
Have another ride on
The replacement bus.

Indigenous folk in what
We'd call Australia
Spied Captain Cook
And cried out hello sailor
But there wasn't much
Chance of cooperation
We'll get Europeans
To build up the nation.

We can send out our
Convicts to save the day
Replacement ships
Off Botany Bay
There's more to come
That's what I'm assuming
Homo erectus becomes
A transhuman.

Some gotta die others
Live for eternity
With Elon Musk
And his jolly fraternity
Upload your brain
Cells into an app
Jettison the body
And all of that crap.

We won't need key workers
Just a few boffins
The rest of you sods
Can relax in your coffins
I live in the penthouse
You skulk in the basement
But we're all getting ready
For the great replacement.

It's all getting closer
Minute by minute
I've seen the future
And I'm not in it
The wise guys are circling
Like pigs at the trough
Please stop the bus
I wanna get off.

WASTE MAN IN THE WASTE LAND

Old Tom Eliot was a right clever dick
When it came to sampling he never missed a trick
He had no compunction and few aversions,
He stole from the Indians, the Greeks and the Persians
The French, the Italians, all rather pathetic
And some of the language was antisemitic.

'April is the cruelest month'. I might have said October
But I go south in winter and come back when I'm sober
'Dare I eat a peach? Or shall I try some prunes?'
I have measured out my life in Wetherspoons
Wasting away in the waste land.

'I think we're in rats' alley
Where the dead men lost their bones'
Where white men steal the blues,
Like Elvis and the Stones.
They did it way back then, they're doing it today
Ed Sheeran got an earful for sampling Marvin Gaye
Let's get it on, it's late in the day.

Everybody's got a hungry heart
But Tennyson with Ulysses got a century's start
Back to old Tom, not too classy with his wife
Put her in an asylum for the rest of her life.

I can saw a woman in two
I didn't write that but neither did you
Made poor Vivien disappear,
For my next trick I'll need a volunteer
Step right up, I'm a slippery man
A waste man in the waste land.

Every move you make, every breath you take
There's a Sting in the tale with royalties at stake,
A whiter shade of pale or a paler shade of grey
Trip the light fantastic and take it away.

'Supine on the floor of a narrow canoe'
I loosened my necktie and thought about you,
Yo, ho, ho and a bottle of rum
Tell Laura I love her but don't tell her mum.

He's just a man of his time, no monster of depravity
He was cool for cats and gave us Macavity,
Broken every human law, now breaks the law of gravity
Top cat in the waste bin, waster in the waste land.

In my beginning is my end
Better stop here or I'll go round the bend,
I'm just a sampling man
Get my lyrics where I can.

CATHOLIC RESCUE

When I say I'm one of nine they think that's plenty
They don't know the half of it, felt more like twenty.

Unwed mums in Ireland had a hard time back then
Put 'em in a convent, you won't see them again.

No contraception, abortion or sex education
Those poor little babes were a blight on the nation.

The Catholic Rescue tried to save the day
Get down to Holyhead and you're on your way.

My mum took them in for months at a time
Till they got sent further down the line.

Another young infant on the mat
Felt more like a commune than a council flat.

No fond farewells , no time to grieve
Don't know if I'll be the next to leave.

I remember their faces , the laughs and the tears
Wonder if I'd know them after all these years.

Did they work on the railway, rid the streets of crime
Some reaching high office, others doing time?

Did they hit it off with their new mums and daddies?
Solid English stock or plastic Paddies.

Maybe they recall the poems from school
An Irish Airman or Wild Swans at Coole.

The Catholic Rescue did what they could
Now Ireland's moved on and that's for the good.

I may catch a glimpse on the tube or the bus
Hope none of the bastards went along with Liz Truss.

These ghost children haunt me, won't let me be
I once was a catholic, come on rescue me.

SOME HAIKUS

A dentist and a
manicurist got married
They fought tooth and nail.

I always thought a
Doppelganger was a type
of German sausage.

Claustrophobich – Russian
Composer who was afraid
To leave home.

Spelt Armageddon wrong
in scrabble final not
the end of the world.

GOOD MOURNING BRITAIN

Lying in a state from a night on the tiles
I saw this queue which was shuffling for miles,
People coming from miles around
For a royal commemoration in London Town.
Started in Bermondsey, then hit the harder stuff
By Tower Bridge I'd had enough
But the crowd was friendly, met me with smiles
I'll do it Charlie . I can queue for miles.
Jump up and down start, start moving around In
for a sovereign, in for a pound.

They're selling postcards of the mourning
Painting the passports blue
The nation's at the crossroads
Half of them in the queue.
Stared at the crowd with
Their banners and pennants
Then a mate came along with
A crateful of Tennant's

Strong stuff for a steady rolling man
At least it does what it says on the can
People got lively, started to sing Rule
Britannia and God Save the King.
I felt out of place, disgruntled and abject
I wanna be a citizen, not a subject
I saw the builder, the baker, the butcher, the boffin
A poor sod got done for touching the coffin.

Saw a prince in uniform
I remember from Woking
Chomping on a pizza
Swore he hadn't been poking,
But he paid out 10 million
Don't know what he'd been smoking
He didn't seem to enjoy the gig
Stiff as a board and sweating like a pig.

Got to the front, avoided a brawl
Just outside Westminster Hall
Got to the door, signing the book
A burly squaddie said sling yer hook
You're out of your head and off your faces
Shouldn't show up in civilized places.

Well, I've seen fire and I've seen rain
Blokes hit on the head with a bicycle chain
But I won't be coming here again.

Went back to the gardens, crashed out by the gate
Spent the whole day lying in state
A right state of grace, as seems to be fitting
Let's raise a glass, good mourning Britain.

HOW THINGS WORK

Never had a clue how things work
You must think I'm a bit of a jerk.

Boiler packed up, that's a bummer
Better call in the Polish plumber.

Can't paint the ceiling or change a tyre
I set up a BBQ but it just caught fire.

Cleaned the windows but still couldn't see clear
As much as I polish there's always a smear.

Can't change a plug or mend a fuse
If you need some rewiring, I'd have to refuse.

Repair the guttering or put up a shelf
My standard response is do it yourself.

When I got a computer, she said right click
I wrote CLICK, Christ, what a dick!

Set up a mousetrap but couldn't catch a mouse
Guess what's needed is a man about the house.

The loft extension left me high and dry
If you need a handyman, I ain't the guy.

I'm not lazy or stupid, well that's my intention
I got second place at the chess convention.

Scrabble and sudoku – I'm shit hot
Poetry prizes, I've got the lot.

Descartes separated the mind from the body
Don't blame me if the workmanship's shoddy.

I don't give a shit about the ghost in the machine
Just need some help when I do the spring clean.

While you fill your head with these fancy ideas
I need an army of volunteers.

If you can't shape up, then get on yer bike
I could write you a poem if you like.

Better be good, we'll see how we go
Amantes para siempre or adios amigo.

IN AND OUT OF AFRICA

I went to the library to pay off my fines
Came out with a copy of King Solomon's Mines
Through the Rift Valley and Great Lakes the staggered
Their bold deeds set down by Easy Rider Haggard.
Then came John Buchan with his pith helmet on
Saving the empire from big Prester John
He pulled the irons out of the fire
And thwarted the plans of the new black messiah.

I learnt of the Congo in all of its vastness
From Mad Mr. Kurtz in the heart of darkness
I followed the explorers as they travelled in style
Like Burton and Speke in their search for the Nile.
Map out the continent and please make it soon
It's Dr Livingstone I presume
But they couldn't get Gordon out of Khartoum.

King's African Rifles in the 1st World War
Signed up by the dozen and died by the score
Fought for the Empire in a place the called home
But weren't even granted a memorial stone
With the colonial mission headed for failure
We needed some names with an African flavour
Like Abubakar Tafawa Balewa.

So I started checking the BBC news
For fierce new leaders with radical views
Like Kwame Nkrumah and Hastings Banda
Good for the goose , fine for the gander.
When Mr. Lumumba got in the way
He was soon sorted out by the CIA
Mandela kept fighting, he couldn't keep silent
Got a life sentence in Robben Island.

The ANC and the MPLA
And ZANU and ZAPU entered the fray,
With Johua Nkomo and Bishop Muzorewa
And of course Abubakar Tafawa Balewa.

At 17 I worked in a store
Just down the road from Kensington Gore
A Saturday job at the illustrious Barker's
I sold a suitcase to a gent from Lusaka.
His name was Kaunda and we had a good natter
About Oginga Odinga and Jomo Kenyatta
A result of my interest was an invitation
To stay at the state lodgings if I came to his nation.
6 years later on August 3rd
President Kaunda was as good as his word.

From Victoria Falls I looked out on Zimbabwe
Civil war raging with comrade Mugabe
I travelled in Kenya with Maasai and Turkana
Picked up Swahili upesi sana.
Saw Jomo speak in Uhuru Park
His raging eyes blazed in the dark
Wananchi thought he saw straight to their heart.

He told about the Mzungu's arrival
When we had the land and they had the bible,
They said 'Kneel down Wananchi and close your eyes
When you awake you'll get a surprise'.

When I lifted my head from out of the sand
We had the bible and they had the land,
I worked there for years, still go back for charity
Sad to see such blatant disparity.

We'll do what we can to see better times
And shake off the burden of King Solomon's Mines.

COCAINE BOOZE AND FIREWORKS

Cocaine, booze and fireworks
Out there with my buddies,
We'll soon have those migrants
Crapping in their chuddies.

Nothing you can do to curb our ambition
If you can't find a paedo, grab a paediatrician
They're trying to take over our way of life
Eye for an eye, gun for a knife.

If you were born here, you're alright
But hold on a minute you need to be white,
We could sit in that hotel drinking whiskey and gin
Take back the Rotherham Holiday Inn.

Get down the mosque and torch it, man
Bring cocaine , booze and fireworks
The shit has hit the fan,
We don't wish to scare you or make a fuss
Just don't like people different from us.

Last war we vanquished our nazi foes
Now we don't seem much different from those,
Arm in the air, fist in the face
We'll soon have you lot out of this place.

This is our country, make no mistake
No foreign food, just burgers and steak
Still, if I can speak with total candour,
I wouldn't say no to a chicken pasanda
If I've had a few and feel under the cosh
I wouldn't turn down a rogan josh.

I go to the Costa for a couple of weeks
But their Spanish practices give me the creeps
I eat my roast dinner in the 40 degree heat.
A day on the sun lounger is my kind of fun
Turning bright red in the afternoon sun,
Time to come home for some peace and quiet
But if the mood takes me, I predict a riot.

I'm not gonna get swallowed up by the pack
You clean the mess up, I'm alright, Jack
Can't beat cocaine, booze and fireworks, can ya?
Let's raise a glass to Cruel Britannia.

CHESSBOARD WARRIORS

They trashed the library, threw rocks at the cops
The mosque wasn't safe and nor were the shops.

Hull has more headbangers than you'd care to mention
Taking their fury out on the chess convention.

Smash all the windows, break down the door
What are you waiting for? Pawn to king 4?

Can't repel us with the Sicilian defence
Knock down your king if you've got any sense.

The captain came out, hands in the air
It's ok mate, sit down in that chair.

I've studied Kasparov and Nimzowitsch on Chess
We'll have a game while they clear up this mess.

I started with white and set out my stall
Best of three, winner takes all.

He started out nervously, had a touch of the shakes
He slowly recovered but a little too late
His queen's gambit failed, three moves and it's mate.

The next two were drawn, so the game was up
I left in triumph clutching the cup.

The cops took my picture, five minutes of fame
A brave chessboard warrior or a pawn in their game?

CARE IN THE COMMUNITY

Solidarity with the heroes of the non-dom community
Giving it large in our land of opportunity
Buy up the houses, both sides of the river
Go south in winter, no need to shiver.

Just park your money, the interest will sort you
Isn't that what your daddy taught you?
Come when you like, it's really no matter
Wimbledon, Ascot, the Henly Regatta.

Pack the kids off to Eton or Harrow
That should keep 'em on the straight and narrow
Party in Chelsea into the night
Everything's cool, the kids are alright.

Gotta do something with this unearned wealth
A spot of grouse shooting on the glorious twelfth?
If all this excitement leads to fatigue
Buy a few clubs in the Premier League.

The big fish are taken but the future's still bright
What about Burnley and Luton tonight?
The last election was a bit of a mystery
The Labour party cast adrift from its history.

Just sit tight and roll up your sleeves
In case we get clobbered by Rachel Reeves
Instead she praised the non-dom community
We might even get diplomatic immunity.

No revolution, no Molotov bombs
You suckers pay taxes, we're the non-doms.

ISLAND OF STRANGERS

A washed-up stranger on a distant shore
In broken English I call through the door
Blissfully oblivious of all of the dangers
Ill-prepared for this island of strangers
They looked at me like I'd strangled a kitten
Broken English in broken Britain
We need to close the migration gap
Start speaking proper like an educated chap.

Get a degree and when the time comes
You'll thrive in a care home wiping our bums
While the country tries to get off its knees
Who'll keep it running while we're at our degrees?

If you think NHS staff won't be missed
Book a year earlier for the waiting list
Long queues at the bus stop, please wait in line
They won't be coming 3 at a time
This isn't the end, we haven't got to the middle
Looks like they're closing another LIDL
Better get ready for a life on the fiddle
I don't think we need all this anxiety
I'd welcome people in all their variety.

It's just a form of self-sabotage
To follow the siren songs of Farage
We're still a rich country, make no mistake
It depends on how we divide up the cake
The fat cats are happy with the current division
The rest of us need to make a decision
Fight over scraps in fair or foul weather
Or repair this broken England together.

Divide and rule, they've learnt it from birth
Our demands are moderate, we just want the earth
Join the struggle, hard as it seems
Turn this island of strangers to an island of dreams.

RECEDING FUTURES

Last year I waltzed off for a tour of Oz
That's the kind of guy I was
Poems in my tucker-bag, fierce and strong
Preach on the beaches and the billabong
But it didn't go well, got dog's abuse
All that sledging, that's no use.

Raw prawns thrown at me in the Barrier Reef
Had to creep off in the night like a thief
Same in Darwin, Perth and Nimbin
Don't want to spend my days in the sin bin
Seem to be setting myself up for failure
Need a total reset to succeed in Australia.

If you're down in the dumps, you better not show it
You can steal the identity of a fellow poet
He's back in London, so he'll never know it
I learnt more from him than all of my teachers
Goes by the name of Redeeming Features.

He has a very sardonic take on life
Not sure I'd leave him alone with my wife
Horse Box Orgies? Just say nay
That went down well in Byron Bay
It wasn't a dead horse we were flogging
They loved the one where Wes goes dogging.

Melbourne to Adelaide, Hobart to Perth
Fans were splitting their sides with mirth
All the gigs were packed to the rafters
Played till 12 and stayed for afters
Under the Southern Cross the stars were gleaming
The beer was flowing, the punters were steaming.

It went to my head, I thought I was dreaming
How many words can you rhyme with redeeming?
The final show was arranged for Sydney
To get a ticket you'd sell a kidney
But the cops stormed in and checked my ID
You're not really who you purport to be.

Just one of those pathetic creatures
Passing yourself off as Redeeming Features
Sitting in the outback doing time
Don't try this at home kids, do juggling or mime
Impersonating a poet is an artistic crime.

WHAT THE DICKENS

My grandchild Sienna is only six
But she seems to be hip to all my tricks
She can tell the difference between
Apple sauce and chutney
When she asks if it's time to
Go to the Putney.

For her Putney is not a location
It's a place for fun and intoxication
A Putney's a pub
But that's ok
It was like that with us
Back in the day.

When I say I grew up in a house without books
I often get some quizzical looks
You must be kidding
I'm sure you had plenty
We had a whole set
Must have been twenty.

Big red volumes, all looked the same
All different titles, one author one name
You'll probably guess
Before the plot thickens
My mum bought a job lot
Of Charlie Dickens.

Off a travelling salesman
On the never never
Should keep us occupied
For ever and ever
They weren't that well-thumbed
But quite well-thrown
He chucked a dickens at me
Was a constant moan.

Ok mum we know what follows
We come from the island of
Saints and scholars
Churchill said of Lenin
Beware the man of one book
Maybe it's time for a closer look
We tossed them around
Playing silly games
The I looked inside and fell in love
With the names.

Bumble and Talkington, Madame Defarge
Mr. Pumblechook giving it large
Wackford Squeers and Mrs. Gamp
Luke Honeythunder sounds delightfully camp
Chuzzlewit and Magwitch out on the town
Leaving Ms Havisham in her wedding gown.

His Child's History of England kept me steady
With Athelstan, Egbert and Ethelred the Unready
Alfred burnt the cakes
But kept the country intact
Till Harold rushed to Hastings
Only to get whacked
By William and his Norman men.

The names started to get boring then
I learnt a lot about language
If only by stealth
I'll pop into a Putney
And drink Charlie's health.

I'll buy you a pint if you lend me a tenner,
Goodnight Sienna.

I COULD LIVE WITH BEING DEAD

I went out surfing in Byron Bay
First wave nearly blew me away
The next one caught me on the hop
Left me flailing all over the shop
Then a monster one, sight unseen
Felt I was spinning in a washing machine
My life passed before me in a blink of an eye
Can't believe I'm going to die

That's your lot mate, took too many risks
But I haven't selected my desert island discs
And what about my funeral songs?
Bet you a tenner you get them all wrong
Old Irish ballads, The Stars and the Plough
Heaven knows I'm miserable now
Better clear these thoughts from my head
On balance I could live with being dead

Avoid chronic pain and losing your mind
Direct me to Dignitas if you'll be so kind
But one thing I'd like before the game's up
To see us win the Double Barrel World Cup
Not the real one, no chance of that
But we'd win the DB at the drop of a hat
Morgan Gibbs-White and Dewsbury-Hall
Sounds like a scene from a debutante's ball
Maitland –Niles and Hudson-Odoi
Alexander-Arnold, he's your boy

Wan-Bissaka and Loftus-Cheek
I'd watch them play every day of the week
I'd like to see the youngsters make the grade
Don't make the same mistakes I made
Gotta make better ones, see how you go
Looks like I'll be the last to know

Oops! Don't know if I was foolish or brave
But in the end I survived the wave
Don't want to look too far ahead
But sometime I'll have to live with being dead
After all this huffing and puffing
Once we had something, now there's nothing.

WHEN THE SAINTS GO MARCHING IN

He wrote his Confessions, rather disgusting
You'd know him better as St Augustine
Made a pact with Jesus, an each way bet
Lord give me chastity, but just not yet!

The patron saint of wine was roasted on a spit
St Vincent raised a glass and said get on with it
Same with St Lorenzo but before he died
Said please turn me over, I'm only done on one side
He's a guy I'd have on my books
Patron saint of comedians and cooks.

St Sebastian was captured but kept up the fight
Assailed by arrows, got pierced by each flight
The ungodly called him a coward, said he died of fright
That human reaction, fight or flight or fright.

St Amandus witnessed some pillage and slaughter
Then spent 15 years on bread and water
But he must have gone on a couple of benders
Ended up the patron saint of bartenders.

St Catherine was offered a deal or no deal
Renounce your faith or die on the wheel
Though she was tempted, she stood her ground
I can still see her whirling around.

St Cassian took up teaching to pay the bills
But every class was a battle of wills
They killed him with writing implements
Possibly quills.

St Patrick sailed off to the Emerald Isle
Converted the natives after a while
Where yer man leads everyone follows
We became the island of saints and scholars
Unlike King Alfred he burnt no cakes
But he rid the island of all of its snakes.

A rock star renowned for shaking his pelvis
Some say they named him after St Elvis
Who didn't croak in the john after too many pills
But baptized St David in the Preseli hills.

St Philip started curing the faithful of snakebite
That's a fierce drink if I have my facts right
The authorities nabbed him as he tried to leave town
And had him crucified upside down.

TALES FROM THE YARD

Passed out at Hendon when I was 19
With a shiny new truncheon and a fistful of dreams,
Bang up the villains and keep the streets clean
Like Dirty Harry and Steve McQueen.

Luther and Dixon, Lewis and Morse
Must be some way to rise in the force,
Proceeding left in a westerly direction
Getting dog's abuse and little affection.

Plodding the beat, soaking wet
Sod this mate, I'm off to the Met
Took the exams and passed the lot
Bright new future, I'll give it a shot
Decent sendoff, everyone pissed
Word in your ear, was there something I missed?

Old sergeant said as I cleared out my locker
Don't come copper on a copper.

Along the mean streets, down in the ditches
Made my contacts, ran my snitches
Saved my arse by the seat of my britches
Fast track promo, back the right horse
A brand new star lights up the force.

Work all hours , no room for skivers
Pushing the envelope full of unmarked fivers
Dig and delve , duck and dive
With AC12 and MI5
Divvy out the takings in a smoky dive
OCG always there with a bung
Scale the ladder rung by rung.

Tell me a porky, I'll tell you a whopper
But don't come copper on a copper.

Jump the ropes, duck through the hoops
Stop right there, don't move or I'll shoot
Go underground, infiltrate a feminist group
Grand new name, big mane of hair
Spread my seed who knows where
Demos and meetings, skirts and blouses
Hard to keep it in my trousers.

Up the duff and down the chute
Not me Guv, I'm outta the loop
Out of my depth, it's getting too hard
Need to get yourself back to the yard
Didn't even leave a calling card.

Might look like a bit of a rotter
But I didn't come copper on a copper.

Get down the clubs, sort out the fights
Have a quick word and shoot out the lights
All night stakeouts, fags and booze
Marriage going down the tubes.

She thought I was a flipper but found I was a flopper
But she didn't come copper on a copper.

Thrills and spills, banter and fun
But a copper's lot's not a happy one
Now I've run out of lives, dobbed in by my mates
Left me hanging by the prison gates
Banged up in the Scrubs, still slopping out
This must be what it's all about.

Looks like I messed up good and proper
And someone came copper on a copper.

DEAD MAN'S SHOES

Popped into the charity shop as I usually do
Got mesmerized by an elegant shoe
Been searching for trainers , Decathlon , JD
Couldn't find anything suitable for me
£30 second hand seemed a bit steep
But they said they'd only been used for a week
After some wear and tear the bloke died in his sleep.

Later that evening I went out for a stroll
And soon found out I was not in control
They took me to places where I'd never been
To the back streets of Croydon to a local shebeen
The music was pumping , such amiable folk
They took me out back for a drink and a smoke
Staggered home at 2, heedful of booze
Walked the last mile in dead man's shoes.

Something is happening, don't know what it is
Looks like I missed my Tuesday pub quiz
Next day I helped out at a homeless shelter
Finished off at the Bedford, the show was a belter
Those shoes took me round on demos and marches
Kipping at the Dorchester or under the arches
Caught the Cirque du soleil , beaucoup de Bonheur
The previous owner was quite a flaneur
Looks like these trainers can't be controlled
Got me into a scrap down the Old Kent Rd

It's a mighty long way from excess to sobriety
When you hang out with the cream and
The dregs of society
Took a bungee jump from the top of the shard
Excuse the brown trousers, this is getting too hard
An exclusive wine tasting, please not one more drop
I'm taking these buggers back to the shop.

Just one more mile, go make that last visit
To see the Lost Souls at the Balham Exhibit
Poems bursting out in all shapes and sizes
No competition, all shall have prizes.

They said you've been around,
Give us one of your own
So I scribbled away and
Came up with this poem.

A WORD IN YOUR EAR

Looks good in a suit, a suitable contender
Should win the election, let's see his agenda
No windfall levy, no taxes on wealth
How we gonna pay for the national health?

Reverse all those cuts in overseas aid
Not quite ready for that I'm afraid
Water companies dump shit in our rivers
I know we should nationalize but it gives me the shivers.

Don't frighten the markets or else we'll be toast
Same with the energy, the trains and the post
Broken Britain, not easy to fix it
And please don't say a word about Brexit.

Das is nicht gut, verstehensie
We really need to talk about Starmzy.

Got to balance the books and look respectable
We'll make some changes but they won't be perceptible
Schools are crumbling, housing in chaos
Fat cats squat on the land awaiting a payoff
But there's no need to get into a spasm
Word of the day is curb your enthusiasm.

Enough to send you for a raid on the pharmacy
We need to have a word about Starmzy.

Rowing back on climate change
When you could be a hero
Nah! We'll take the slow lane to net zero
Steady as you go, don't go on a bender
Never learnt the words to Hey Big Spender.

Some want him soaked in a butt of Malmesey
That's from Shakespeare, you may know it slightly
Or I'm just wearing my learning lightly
Yes it's time to have a word with Starmzy.

BOMBDOG MILLIONAIRE

You ain't nothing but a ground dog,
Yapping all the time
Snapping at our heels,
Keeping us in line
Get grief from fans
At Brentford and Fulham
Not allowed bite so I
Push 'em and pull 'em
There's a couple of arseholes
Down from the bar
Kicking up a rumpus over VAR
Looks like something's going
On in the bog
No, it's only a couple
Having a snog
Saw a young lad with
A teargas canister
Chased him downstairs as
He slid down the banister
They pat my head and
Give me some treats
But I wish I could sit
In the executive seats.

I remember the days at
White Hart Lane
Sniffing the banknotes for
A trace of cocaine
Can't see the game as
I'm faced the other way
Every game seems like
Groundhog day
But the post came today
And I got a surprise
If I could read I wouldn't
Believe my eyes
The card seemed like
A royal invitation
Looks like I'm working
At the coronation
Got a makeover,
My fur was glistening
A marching band played but
No one was listening
Folk had come from all
Over the shop
To cheer on a pensioner
Who got his first job
The Queen liked her corgis,
The King likes Camilla

I'd go for a greyhound like
Mick the Miller
I got a call,
Hairs started to bristle
No one else heard it,
Was a dog whistle
This is the moment to
Go the whole hog
Feel like a tadpole
Turned into a frog
You're a bomb dog now
Go sniff out the danger
There's something odd about
That devious stranger
The fiend had explosives,
A threat to the nation
I jumped up to foil
A royal assassination
He came at me,
His eyes full of malice
But I leapt up and chased him
All round the palace
I got decorated,
Invited my mates
Who let the dogs in?

Best shut the gates
Maybe I'm getting
Above my station
But I'm the bombdog
Who saved the nation
Next season at Luton,
Promotion in sight
Burnley too,
They're up for the fight
Every dog has his day and
Bob Marley was right
Gonna be Burnley an'
A Luton tonight

MORE SAINTS

St Jude does lost causes, St Christopher lost keys
St Ambrose honey, looks after the bees
Santa Cecilia, I'm down on my knees
She's the patron of music but knows every art
You're shaking my confidence,
You're breaking my heart.

If your family gives you the heave-ho
Get on your knees and pray to St Ivo
If you're a youngster on the skids
He's the saint of abandoned kids
Get yourself housed but when you do
Remember he's the saint of landlords too.

Catherine of Sweden, I'd treat her with caution
She wants to protect young girls from abortion
If you need one, she's opposed I'm afraid
Wants to abolish Rowe versus Wade
I thought that was a debate about crossing a river
But she's out there ready to stand and deliver.

St Gertrude will protect you from mice
If you're infested, go take her advice
Got a nice name, could be German
Maybe she's handy with all kinds of vermin
Do a job lot for bedbugs and lice
Sure she can bend them all to her will
And go the distance with Rentokil.

If you have gangrene or a similar disease
Or need your legs cut off at the knees
St Antonio of Padua you won't need to beg
And it won't cost you an arm and a leg
This skilful surgeon charged minimum fees
He's the patron saint of amputees.

Show me the whisky stains on the floor
Show me the drunkard as he stumbles out the door
Bless me father for I have sinned
I got pissed and I got binned.

Got my collar felt by the plod
Last hope is St John of God
A night in the cells and I'll go clear
Spend no more money on whisky and beer
Thank you John of God , I wouldn't talk bollocks
To the patron saint of alcoholics.

St Zeno came from Africa, a bit of a loner
But he worked his way up to Bishop of Verona
The people were pleased , made him saint of the city
But a few xenophobes started acting shitty
Didn't want a black man as their local saint
Looks rather fascistic, correct me if it ain't.

St Cantilupe brought to life a dead hawk
Then taught a tongueless man to talk
It seems it had been cut out by a felon
Anyway, enjoy your cantaloupe melon

BORN TO Q

I remember the days when music was free
Festivals funded by the GLC
Clapham Common had reggae and blues
Bring your own food and take in some booze.

Salsa all day at the Elephant and Castle
Keep in time, don't be an arsehole
I was a multicultural big time
Charlie Cool for Hanukkah,
Eid and Diwali.

Forget about all that burning an a looting
It's Rock against Racism and freedom for Tooting.

Marley at the Round House up in Chalk Farm
The aroma of sensi did me no harm.

No online booking, just splash the cash
Catch the Pogues, the Jam and the Clash.

Now it's all corporate hospitality
Seems like I'm losing my grip on reality.

Off to see Springsteen, a day in Hyde Park
100 smackers, should be a lark.

But I couldn't retrieve the Q code on my phone
Looks like I'm heading for the twilight zone.

They frisked my bags but I didn't get felt
I sneaked a hip flask under my belt.

But my home made sarnies didn't get in
And my fake Ribena went into the bin.

They even impounded my polo mints
They wouldn't do that to Beyonce or Prince.

We've a no food policy, it's written down there
But Polos aren't sustenance, they're mostly air.

It's more than my job's worth, end up on the dole
Ok, you take the mints, I'll have the hole.

Let's get in there and have some fun
Some are born to Q code, I'm born to run.